BEYOND THE BILLBOARDS

Truth About Great Customer Service

Turning Promises into Reality

Michael J. Crain

authorHOUSE®

AuthorHouse™
1663 Liberty Drive, Suite 200
Bloomington, IN 47403
www.authorhouse.com
Phone: 1-800-839-8640

First published by AuthorHouse 12/6/2007

ISBN: 978-1-4343-2663-8 (e)
ISBN: 978-1-4343-2661-4 (sc)
ISBN: 978-1-4343-2662-1 (hc)

Printed in the United States of America
Bloomington, Indiana

This book is printed on acid-free paper.

Acknowledgment

To my wonderful wife Carla, son C.J. and daughter Kelsey thanks for your love, support and amazing ability to deal with dad's crazy addiction to research.

To the brilliant Lesley Lovallo, Bruce Benson, Robbyn McDowell, Michelle Clark, Daniel Nino, Jon Lineback, and team, thanks for keeping pace and setting me straight when my aim was off.

While audibly your voice went silent much too young, know Mom your spirit is loud and clear. Thanks for instilling belief.

Contents

Part Four
SO SIMPLE IT'S DIFFICULT

Part Five
THE LEADERSHIP PARADOX

FOREWORD

"Why is it that so many organizations spend galactic amounts of money on advertising, trying to seduce people to visit, shop, fly or stay, yet so little time and effort ensuring people get what they've been promised?"

A member of the audience asked this question during a strategy workshop I was conducting, and due to the groans from the crowd, I knew the majority shared her opinion. Common sense suggests that if you make a claim to provide prompt and caring customer service, you should deliver what you promise. At least that's what all those groans of dissatisfied customers suggested to me.

For example, the travel industry (according to one of the leading resources of advertisement insights, *Advertising Age*) spent more than $5.4 billion on advertising, and yet how many airlines actually offered flights anything close to their claims? If you frequently travel around America on airplanes, particularly if you fly economy, you know the answer to that. The same goes for many rental car agencies and hotel chains. Cellular phone companies spent more than $10.9 billion, and the automotive industry spent $19.7 billion attempting to grab our attention. Invariably many claimed, in some form or fashion, to provide congenial, fair, helpful customer service—to the tune of $36 billion spent in total advertising. So what were all those groans in the audience about? Why are you shaking your head right now?

American consumers know that great service is the exception, not the rule, today. When we encounter it in reality, rather than in a glamorous TV commercial or on a glossy magazine page, we are surprised and grateful. We tell our friends about it. We reward the company with our repeat business.

Unfortunately we can't quantify the amount of money (and time) spent on ensuring the execution of what was promised by those catchy jingles and pretty faces, but common sense tells us that most companies didn't spend nearly enough money on their performance compared to the millions they spent on advertising.

There are exceptions, of course. There are companies that do honor their promises and match their pledges with great customer service. While small in number, they bask in the rare glow of consumer confidence. Their brands flourish and their profits grow.

For more than fifteen years now, I have been studying the corporate landscape from this perspective by contrasting corporate overachievers with the under-performers. In the early years, I did so out of pure curiosity, but for the last seven years, my curiosity has turned into a professional obsession. I almost consider an encounter with a company that provides thoughtful, good-natured service as a romantic affair. No kidding. My heart skips a beat when I find an organization that consistently and genuinely cares for its patrons.

Once I find one of these lovely companies, I unashamedly stalk them. I observe their daily routines and their leadership initiatives, eager to find out what makes them so *beautiful* in the eyes of consumers. How do they manage to remain so radiantly profitable and productive? I'm almost euphoric when I discover the basic underlying facts that explain how these companies have achieved and maintained such strikingly attractive personalities.

Today I have a team of dedicated, clever people who assist me in this never-ending quest for information about the highest-achieving organizations in our country and our world. With their help I have gained a wealth of valuable insights about the reality of great customer service.

The pages that follow contain many of these insights. Most were discovered simply by contrasting the actual performances of those who preach good customer service with those who truly practice it. We did not restrict our research to any one particular sector but opted to examine numerous industries. Our goals were, first, to discover the commonalities shared by the most successful companies and, secondly, to determine how they differed from their direct competitors. Of course we collected an abundance of data, but **the essence of our research can be reduced to a few basic principles, principles shared by all highly successful companies and organizations.**

Finally we found that the implementation of these basic principles can be measured on a daily basis. **As a result, every company can establish its own straightforward, reliable system of accountability when it comes to customer service.**

For nearly ten years, I served as director of corporate development for an aviation, real estate, and auto retail management company. With more than fifty years of business under our belt and annual revenue hovering at a billion dollars a year, it would have been easy to become complacent. However, our founder had always been unyielding in his determination to avoid corporate complacency and self-indulgence. Happy? Yes. Satisfied? Never.

Relentlessly, under his leadership, we searched for ways to improve our performance, and with each improvement, our organization grew. The organization still has room to improve and grow, but the knowledge it has applied thus far has greatly influenced profits, production, and most importantly, the satisfaction of its consumers. Naturally its employees are very pleased as well, but never self-satisfied.

This book is for all those executives who strive for customer satisfaction as if it were a holy grail, one that could provide everlasting success. It is for those who want to do more than plaster billboards with seductive slogans or print logos on the pages of newspapers, or broadcast slick TV commercials, or babble empty promises over radio.

The media offers powerful means to acquire customer recognition, but it carries a serious risk as well. If your claims, broadcast at great expense, turn out to be false—if your customer's actual experience betrays your ad promises—then all the recognition your company has purchased can easily turn to resentment, even anger.

This is a book for executives who understand that ten angry customers can do more harm to a business than a hundred billboards or a dozen TV commercials can ever undo.

If you understand that, then I'm confident you'll find the following pages both useful and rewarding.

PART ONE

A COMMON-SENSE APPROACH TO CUSTOMER SERVICE

1. A Lesson from a Samurai

Reaching the top—whether in the Rockies or in business—isn't always easy, and staying there is even more difficult.

After graduating in 1985, I purchased my first brand-new vehicle, a Suzuki Samurai. I was very proud and took it anywhere and everywhere, showing it off to anyone who would give me the opportunity. Keep in mind it's a very simple vehicle. "A tiny tin box wrapped in aluminum foil," was how a not-so-impressed friend described it, but to me it was made of gold—gold in a teal green sort of way—with a gray interior and white spoke wheels. Naturally he was never allowed to ride in my small chariot again.

Soon after I purchased the Samurai, my girlfriend and her parents invited me to accompany them to their timeshare in Colorado, where they went to ski for a week every year. Of course I gladly accepted their invitation, but on one condition: that we be allowed to follow her parents in my Samurai. I didn't want to ride in their Volvo. After all, I had a Suzuki!

The day came to travel. As we crossed through Texas, the tip of Oklahoma, and into Colorado, all was going well until we hit the Rocky Mountains. Suddenly I began to realize the not-so-subtle differences between my small car and their Volvo. It soon became evident that the engineers at Volvo had a little more—excuse me, a lot more experience—when it came to engineering a car for difficult, steeply-graded terrain. The Volvo seemed to mock the Samurai as it cruised effortlessly up the mountain ahead of me.

I had to keep it in third gear because, if I put it in fourth, it would begin to tumble backwards. Even in third it struggled mightily. At one point, we were moving so slowly that a hitchhiker with a sixty-pound backpack could have outrun us. This was all embarrassing, to say the least—especially because my girlfriend and her father had switched places just before the climb began. With our shoulders only separated by a few inches, my blushes became acute. Trying to be discrete, her father pushed himself back into the passenger seat and slowly turned his head to the left to verify that I was giving it gas. Staring straight out the windshield, I said in a helpless voice, "Sir, I'm giving it all she's got." And while he would never admit it, I swore he said under his breath, "And you're dating my daughter?"

As we made it to the summit of each mountain, the Samurai would audibly gasp for air. So would I, and then would floor it down the other side, hoping to gain as much momentum as possible before we began to struggle up the next peak. We finally made it to their timeshare, but for the rest of the week I was full of dread about our return journey to Texas. As it turned out, we eventually arrived home safely, and along with my lingering embarrassment and a new appreciation for miracles, I had learned an important life lesson.

The Samurai had taught me that the landscape of life always changes. Vast flatland can induce a false sense of security. In central Texas, where the highest elevation you'll normally contend with is a highway interchange, you may gain all sorts of confidence—but that confidence turns out to be counterfeit. My youthful encounter with the Rocky Mountains made it clear to me that life's terrain can suddenly change. Inevitably life is going to present you with a challenge that you naively failed to realize even existed.

This lesson, I believe, certainly applies to business. I've seen more organizations than I can count rise and fall because the owners or executives felt as if their business was going to continue running as smoothly, as easily, as a drive across Texas—**until new competition appeared on the horizon, and they weren't prepared to elevate their customer service to new heights of performance.**

When the business was moving on familiar ground, they looked at their P&L statements, stock prices, and/or customer counts and thought everything was going to continue just as it had in the past. In other words, they failed to see the change in their market until it was too late. Their formerly successful business suddenly was laboring and straining like my little Samurai, just trying to keep up.

2. FACTS, NOT FICTION

Customers believe what they experience, day by day, not what they are told in advertisements.

As a young consultant for a global organization with a long history of exponential growth, I saw firsthand a company doomed by its own complacency. Quite suddenly the competition jacked up their performance by a factor of ten. It wasn't very long before we were struggling to keep up with them.

As in many large organizations, the staff had seen this coming first, but the executive leadership at corporate headquarters, isolated within their lavish corner offices, was satisfied with the status quo for much too long. They never acknowledged the need to develop a new strategy. At staff meetings the phrase "We will stick with what has propelled this company for the past twenty years" became a kind of tribal chant. This chant would eventually begin to sound like a funeral dirge accompanying the company's slow, painful loss of its market dominance.

Unfortunately none of those executives had read *Good to Great* by Jim Collins. This book is rich in research and penetrating insight about the steps a business must take in order to develop an organization from good to great or even from bad to good. One of Collins's most profound findings deals with how to face the "brutal facts" of your reality.

Many companies fail to reach their full potential because the executives refuse to see the real gaps in their day-to-day performance—especially when it comes to their customer service. Instead of dealing with facts, unsuccessful leaders prefer to believe their own fiction.

Instead of being dedicated to constantly improving service, they choose to rest on last year's performance and believe that momentum will carry them through the next challenge. The next challenge to any company is the very next customer to walk through the door.

Proof of this is not difficult to find. Simply reflect on your last few encounters with a car dealership, bank, insurance company, dry cleaner, restaurant, gas station, car rental agency, grocery store, or airline. How many promises about friendly, caring, helpful service have these organizations given to you over the years? How many of them actually delivered something extraordinary in the way of service the last time you gave them your business?

As I was writing the introduction to this book, I heard a radio commercial for a national insurance company whose tag line was...

"Call 1-800-BLAH-BLAH-BLAH and get the customer service you deserve."

After the commercial aired four times in two hours, I picked up the phone and called the number. After three rings I got the familiar recorded robot voice saying, "Your call is important to us. All calls are answered in the order they were received. Thank you for your patience." Then five minutes of irritatingly bland elevator music followed until my call was actually answered by a human drone posing as a customer service rep.

In a monotone voice of boredom, she said, "Thank you for calling XYZ Insurance. How may I help you?" at which point I thought, *If this is the service I deserve, what did I do so wrong?*

I wondered what the chances were that those executives who had signed off on this national, million-dollar ad campaign had ever dialed the number to verify the service they were promising. Had they done it before airing the ad? Before writing the huge check to the advertising agency? How many seconds would it have taken them?

With this in mind, I did a little research and identified the president of the company, then wrote him a gentle letter of inquiry that I guessed would receive at least a polite response. After two weeks and no reply to my handwritten letter, I e-mailed him four times in six weeks. Can you guess how long it took to finally get a response? I'm still waiting.

Unfortunately for all of us today, few things are more common than a business making a grand promise about customer

service without the systems in place to actually deliver on that promise. Just ask any consumer. Just recall your own experiences.

I was hosting a customer focus group when an articulate participant made the following statement about companies and their advertising: "A lie is anything, said or unsaid, done with the intent to deceive." He was making the point that many organizations simply are lying in the face of consumers by promising one thing but delivering another—by offering seductive slogans without any substance.

Later I asked for a few minutes of his time and asked whether he sincerely believed that most companies were out to deceive the public.

"No, but too many companies are either guilty of lying or guilty of consumer negligence. **Making a promise without validating your ability to deliver is negligence.** When they advertise, in essence they're trying to adopt my personal business. Shouldn't they make certain their house is in order, so when I visit them, I can see they are worthy candidates to parent my business? If I do show up and invest time and energy, but discover that they really couldn't care less about me, isn't that customer negligence?" His rhetorical question made a huge impact.

3. MEASURE YOUR CUSTOMER PERFORMANCE

National rankings on customer service are no substitute for the three kinds of comparisons you should make yourself.

During my years in corporate development, I have spoken to audiences from Boston to Portland, from Texas to Minnesota. I've faced small teams huddled around boardroom tables and large crowds at civic centers and banquet halls. My talks have primarily been attended by executives and owners. In preparing for such events, I often ask what they expect to gain from my presentation. One of the most common answers is they want the knowledge needed to grow consumer confidence in order to obtain market-share dominance.

As the session begins, I often ask my audience to define what they mean by customer satisfaction. Many passionately respond about their commitment to being the best provider of fast, fair, and friendly service. After all their sincere pledges, I ask, "How many *advertise* in any form that you're a provider of fast, fair, and friendly service?"

The majority raise their hands, nod, or respond with an audible confirmation. Pressing further I asked "How many of you believe that your service is better than most?" Most proudly display their confidence.

I then asked "How many in the last seventy-two hours have *emotionally* put yourself in the consumers' shoes as you observed a transaction taking place?"

"How many in the last thirty days have called in through an unidentifiable phone line and played the role of customer—in order to experience the treatment a caller receives?"

"How many have then called your competition to assess how much better—or worse—you are?"

At this point, many in my audience take their eyes off me and find something else to look at. Having been in their seat before, I know that such behavior indicates an attempt to escape—not from my gaze but from their own guilty consciences.

Just like I was prior to 1994, many in my audience are looking for a big, fancy box that contains the Grand Idea for improving their customer service performance. In fact, the truth comes in a simple package of common sense. If we want consumer confidence that yields additional market share, we need not look much further than our current customers. I am not saying that media advertising or business strategy is insignificant. Still, they are not nearly as important as current performance.

Likewise, common sense says that observing your current transactions from a customer's perspective is a better measurement of your service than relying on national rankings. I have seen high rankings cripple a company's ability to deal with their deficiencies and blind them to the greater possibilities that immediate improvements can bring.

Many organizations validate their own performance by using rankings provided by independent resources like *Forbes, Money Magazine*, Gallup, and J.D. Power. While these independent sources do provide beneficial data, they should not be the sole means by which we measure the service our company provides. J.D. Power, for example, does an exceptional job at ranking companies, but being named number one by J.D. Power does not necessarily mean you're *distinctively* different or have *exceptional* customer service. It can—and too frequently does—highlight the best of the worst.

If a study of ten companies is conducted and all have mediocre performance, someone may be recognized as "the winner" and be tempted to beat their proverbial chest as they make their way to center stage. But this celebrated status can be a farcical self-delusion based on "outstanding" customer service that in reality is no more than a comparatively modest accomplishment.

Comparing national rankings can be interesting and constructive, but there are other comparisons that prove to be far more valuable.

During our quest for the principles and strategies behind truly effective performance, we looked at proven companies like Southwest Airlines, GE, Starbucks, Marriott, QuikTrip, In and Out Burger, and Nordstrom's, to name just a few. We established three critical areas of comparison. We call these **self comparison, industry comparison** and **ultimate possibility comparison.** I will be explaining each in detail in "Part Three: Dimensions of Comparison," but first I want to ensure that you are convinced of the absolute importance of measuring your company's performance on a continual basis. After all, winning an Olympic gold medal doesn't guarantee that you will be the fastest runner in your next race, and every NFL player knows that a Super Bowl ring may earn him everlasting respect, but it won't win the next game for his team. Performance in business is no different. Your company's service is only as effective as your next customer.

PART TWO

THE COMMITMENT TO CONTRAST

Great Is the Company That Has the Courage
to Compare

1 . The Room in Our Mind

Opening the Door to the Truth of Our Reality

While sitting in an office waiting for a fellow executive, I notice a quote engraved on a wooden pencil holder:

"Happiness is found when you don't feel the need to compare."

Within limits I might agree, but this point of view is far too close for comfort to another old bromide, "Ignorance is bliss." Who wants that kind of happiness, based on self-deluded complacency? Since I knew the person who occupied this office rather well, I was not surprised to find this piece of "wisdom" on his desk. The guy's performance matched his "philosophy" to a painful degree.

The organizations and people I've enjoyed working with, or those I respect after much research, all dare to compare and contrast their performance with that of their competitors. Jack Welch, the famed CEO of General Electric, for example, achieved phenomenal success for his company by insisting on knowing how well it measured up to the competition.

Here's an even more dramatic example from history. One of Churchill's great advantages over Hitler was that he insisted on facing up to the reality of his situation and monitored the British performance in WWII on a daily, even hourly basis. In contrast, anyone who dared to bring bad news to Hitler—news that in any way contradicted his deluded claims of global domination—was very likely to suffer terrible consequences. Churchill appointed an intelligence committee whose only job was to provide tough, unedited, realistic facts about how Britain was performing in comparison to its Nazi enemies. History proves that contrasting one's performance and dealing with harsh truths can make all the difference between winning or losing, life or death.

Having conducted many one-on-one sessions, strategy meetings and training seminars, I've concluded that one of the common flaws found in underperforming individuals and organizations is a lack of self-awareness. Think of a person you know who has a serious flaw in their personality (or strategy). While the flaw is clear to everyone else, the individual himself consistently fails to see it. This kind of "perceptional defense" can be likened to a closed room in the mind, a room that contains all the vivid truth of our reality but whose door remains closed to many people.

In my experience, every one of us has a room like this and the potential to open its door and enter. Of course, we all differ in how often we open that door and step inside. Unfortunately there are too many people who never dare to confront the total reality of their own lives.

When you actively compare your behavior to your core values, or contrast your organization's performance to that of others, it's hard to escape seeing where you have fallen short in terms of execution. All the claims about personal commitment can quickly be revealed to be more "slogan" than substance.

I founded Performance Architects, LLC to work alongside organizations that sincerely desired to move forward in the area of customer relations. One of our most important techniques, offered after we complete our training, is what we call "mystery shops." In these, one or more of my team will arrive at our client's business playing the role of an interested consumer, equipped with a hidden "button" camera and microphone in order to record an authentic customer's perspective. We also do "phone shops" and record them. We undertake these exercises both to validate the effectiveness of our training and to provide clear evidence of our client's performance.

One of our clients asked us to work with both their sales and service divisions. After conducting extensive training, we offered one free round of mystery shops. The executives leading the service division jumped out of their seats with a *yes*. In contrast, the sales executives almost disappeared beneath their seats. Why? The sales division had always claimed to offer superior leadership and customer service, but they had few, if any, systems in place to validate this. They feared their own promises wouldn't stand up in reality.

On another occasion we conducted a mystery shop at a major electronics superstore that proudly claimed, on conspicuous yellow wall posters, to deliver an experience that you would want to tell your friends about. After our mystery shop, we presented our recorded DVD to the management. Instead of concentrating on the hideous customer service we had captured on video, they chose to concentrate on the fact that we didn't have written prior authorization. As of the writing of this book, they remain mired in poor customer service and plummeting consumer confidence. Indeed, often when I'm in a public forum speaking about customer service, people will volunteer their own "worst experiences"—often at this chain of electronics super stores!

Thirty days after our first mystery shop at this electronics store, I returned to the store myself. The service was, if anything, even worse, although the posters had been removed. This is a sad but not uncommon example of an organization. Once outstanding, it descends into the realm of mediocrity or even notoriety. It always amazes me when I encounter management whose stubborn refusal to face reality is blatantly obvious to everyone but themselves. Of course, when the inevitable catastrophe strikes their business, the last ones they will blame will be themselves.

2. Keep Your Eye on the Customer

Top Executives Share the Same Realistic Values

Take a look at Scott Holland, the sales and marketing vice president of Taylor Woodrow Homes, a global home builder whose slogan is "Homes Inspired by You."

Holland and his team have been experiencing exceptional growth. Along with their successful results, they have won one customer service award after another. While being interviewed about the reasons for his firm's success, Holland said,

"We're dedicated to hiring the right people, developing our people, and validating our performance by contrasting it—not only to our core values but to the performance of our competitors."

He then leaned forward and with determination in his voice said, "Our mission is to genuinely keep our customers at the center of our attention. Our dedication to doing so is the reason we succeed."

Bruce Benson of EMC shares the same goals. EMC is a company with a long history of market-share dominance. Like Taylor Woodrow, they can cover several large walls with the multitude of customer service awards they've won. When responding to my questions about why his team continues to out-perform their competition, Benson replied, "We, unlike many in the industry, have tenured employees. Our team is determined to develop their customer service skills to the point that they can turn every customer into an advocate. We spend a lot of time and money on customer service, leadership, and personal development. We review our performance, not only with the aid of manufacturers' survey's results, but also with frequent mystery shops. We can develop all we want, but if it doesn't impact the experience from the customer's point of view, and we're no different than our competition, we're not going to make true progress in our business."

Jack Welch vowed to make GE either number one or two in each of its business sectors or else quit that sector. The only way to know if you're accomplishing a mission like this is, of course, to continually measure your performance in comparison to that of your competition. It was a bold proclamation by Welch, but his strategy paid off. GE became known as "the best led company on the face of the planet."

What about your organization? **To what extent do you measure your daily performance in customer service? How often do you compare your company's actual customer interactions with those of your competitors? On a personal level, how often do you compare your daily routine to your strategic goals**?

Only when we actually measure our performance using the standard of direct comparison—the only standard by which human performance can be accurately gauged—do we open the door to that room in our mind where reality can be seen objectively and clearly. There we can leave behind the dangers of self-destructive ignorance and view the truth about our life and our business.

3. Prepare to Perform

Ask a Few Key Questions Before You Make Public Promises

I was invited to an executive meeting where two wholesale conglomerates had merged in order to merge their talent pool. The objective was to develop a new business plan with a strong sales strategy in order to take full leadership of their market. At this meeting a strategy was presented about how to infiltrate their competitors' territory. My attendance was requested as an objective critic of their plans, but all the signs showed me that what they were really after was my uncritical affirmation.

The room was arranged in a U-shaped format, giving me a clear view of all their flipcharts, PowerPoint presentations, and eager faces. Each executive spoke passionately about going "head to head" with the competition, about getting "face to face" with the competitors' clients. They would win this new territory by convincing everyone that they were superior in service.

After listening for ninety minutes, I was invited to comment. I stepped up to the podium and for several minutes congratulated them all on their dynamic, inspirational presentation. Then I asked *the question*.

"From all that I've heard today, your strategy for growing market share is based on sending your sales and marketing force out to inform the public about your superiority in customer service. You are going to vow to take far better care of your customers than the companies with whom they're currently doing business."

Everyone in the room nodded.

"How do you know?"

Evidently asking those four words—"How do you know?"—can instantly evaporate the oxygen within a boardroom. There was an audible gasp from all thirty-two executives around the big U-shaped table. Several more minutes of stunned silence passed until one bold executive proclaimed, "Michael, we're faster and more proficient than our competition. We have better response times and friendlier, more attentive customer service agents."

"And to add to that," another executive chimed in, "the fact that we've assembled a great team of managers to run our operations." A wave of nodding heads went around the table.

"Okay," I said, "so you're going to go out and capture market share by telling your prospective clients that you're better at response times, customer service, and management. How do you know? **Have you placed an order with your current competitors and**

then placed one with your own company and timed both responses?

"Have you called your competitor and placed an order and then called your own company and placed an order to validate the difference in customer care?

"Better yet, have you called and filed a complaint with your competitor? Then done the same with your own company and noted the difference in the two responses?

"Have you contrasted the effectiveness of your Web site to that of your competition?

"Have you researched or met with executives from the competition in order to validate your own superiority in terms of leadership?

"What are the real differences between you and your competition in terms of training and ongoing leadership development?"

Unfortunately it's far too common today for a company to claim they're "better" or "the best" without any proof. Just because we have strong ambitions and good people, that alone does not make us better than our competition.

After all, they too feel "better," feel confident of their own good people. Being good does not automatically make an organization better than the competition. In fact, being "good" normally equates to being the same as everyone else. If we as a company claim to be better, doesn't that already make us the same? Our competition is making the identical claim. By advertising and promoting our service as being "better," we have to dare to compare and to contrast if we are to ensure our claim is true and not another example of consumer negligence.

While my questions were not popular at first, they served their purpose. The gathered executives agreed to postpone the kickoff date until they were able to validate that they indeed had the people and processes in place, to gather the proof of their superiority. The result was a successful launch and an effective customer service program that today stands at the top of its industry.

PART THREE

DARE TO COMPARE

Three Kinds of Comparisons Leading to
Outstanding Performance

1. Self Comparison

Mirror, mirror on the wall, are we living up to our promises?

Self comparison occurs when we contrast what we believe with what we actually do. In the corporate world, this means comparing a mission statement to the company's daily performance. All too often companies spend hours in boardrooms crafting mission statements but give little consideration to the means by which they will be achieved. When performance benchmarks are suggested, they are frequently too superficial.

A company whose mission statement promises to deliver outstanding customer service often has no other benchmarks than gross revenue, stock value, or the number of products sold. In fact, these could also be the result of an advertising campaign or of business location, or a combination of factors. Such benchmarks fail to focus specifically on the delivery of outstanding customer service.

In seventeen of the twenty convenience store companies that we researched, there was a promise of a fast, friendly experience. Take a look at ten examples of what we found:

Circle K "Our stores are known around the world for offering busy customers a wide variety of quality products and services in a fast, friendly, and clean environment."

Exxonmobil/On the Run "People who recognize you, who add a little sparkle … fast, fresh and friendly."

Flying J "We are committed to … providing premium hospitality."

AM/PM "At AM/PM you will find commitment to excellence and an emphasis on respect in how we treat our customers and each other. AM/PM offers a fast, fun, dynamic and rewarding environment."

7-Eleven "At the core of our business are the customers… our commitment to give them what they want, when and where they want it."

QuikTrip "When you walk into a QuikTrip convenience store, you immediately know you're somewhere special. The people are friendly and helpful."

Wawa "Our core values … delight customers."

E-Z Mart "It is the mission of E-Z Mart to provide customers with quality products and services in a friendly, convenient manner."

And so on, and on, *ad nauseum.*

Of the ten mentioned above, few actually had systems in place to measure "friendliness." Yet it only takes one visit to an outstanding store like QuikTrip to feel the difference.

Such companies do more than print cheerful posters. They actually measure their hospitality. Their commitment to congenial service extends to their own employees, helping QuikTrip to be ranked twenty-one on Fortune's list of Top 100 companies to work for in 2006.

How many gas stations have left you feeling as if you were more than just a means to their revenue, a faceless transaction completed? Based on your own observations, how many convenience chains have a truly selective hiring practice? How many times have you walked out thinking the salesperson actually cared about your business? Visit the Web site of your local convenience store and then compare that with your own experience. Unfortunately, if you do so, you will have done more than many convenience chain CEO's ever do.

I have used convenience stores as an example here, but we could replace them with department stores, medical clinics, or building supply warehouses and reach the same conclusions. While certainly there are organizations that perform self-comparisons, the majority do not, and that's precisely why so many never rise above the ordinary. Sitting in the comfort of company headquarters, watching the stock market, does not keep the core values of an organization alive and well.

Just how beneficial would it be for the owner/executive of a company to spend half an hour every month contrasting their mission statement to the reality of their performance? Not hours a week or weeks a month but just half an hour a month. There are 43,200 minutes in an average month, so investing thirty of them in such an exercise would seem to be a prudent way for someone to move their operations a little closer to reality. What facts would surface? In my experience, they would be important if *seemingly trivial* facts that could help bring the company in line with its public promises.

As simple as it seems, too few executives recognize the need for regular self-comparisons. At worst, they are like the CEO of a national trucking and warehousing company I once interviewed. "The mission statement," he said. "That's just something we could put on our Web site. It means nothing." One year later, unsurprisingly, he was fired.

Let's contrast him to Stephen Burd of Safeway. In 2004, we began to research the Safeway grocery store chain. Back in 1992, the company had almost gone under. Yet, two years later, under Burd's leadership, it ranked fourth in national sales. By 2004, that number had reached an excess of $35 billion. Noting this fantastic turnaround, we began to probe their business philosophy and corporate structure. It didn't take long to realize how many ways CEO Stephen Burd had helped to save Safeway, to orchestrate their expansion and, most importantly, to develop a truly customer-sensitive culture. Safeway now has more than 1,800 stores and has evolved dynamically thanks to Burd's development of people and processes, including the implementation of a "mystery shop" program.

Burd is known for a passion to please customers, for measuring performance and instituting bonus programs for staff high-achievers. During one of our Safeway interviews, Russell Wolfe, a member of Burd's management team, said, "We're not just hopeful that our staff members, me included, are participating in the daily practices that ensure customer satisfaction. We monitor this through programs that regularly assess how Safeway achieves its stated objectives, in order to turn our buyers into returning customers."

Recently Performance Architects completed a round of 27 focus groups, with more than 154 consumers attending. One interesting finding was the discovery that many people enter a business just to validate the company's slogan. Basically they are actively trying to negate its claims. One man told us, "I go in expecting bad service. I'm actually looking for ways to prove their dishonesty. I'm in disbelief when I find a place that delivers what they promise." As we conducted these sessions, such consumer cynicism surfaced time and time again. Our conclusion was obvious. More than ever before, companies today need the courage to compare their daily activity to their promises in order to recapture the trust of the buying public.

Self-comparison is essential for personal growth as well. Picture, for a moment, a sheet of legal paper in landscape format. On the far left bottom corner, there's a dot representing where you are today. Let's attach an annual income figure of $50,000. On the far right lower corner is another dot representing where you will be in five years. Again we'll put *$50,000*. Then move up the right side about halfway and put another dot with *$100,000* next to it. Another dot is now placed in the far upper-right-hand corner with *$200,000*. In five years we could be at the same annual income level or have risen above to $200,000 and beyond. The difference in income and lifestyle would be dramatic, but only a small degree of change is needed today to put your life on a life-changing trajectory. Making a commitment today and remaining committed can produce an enormous difference over time.

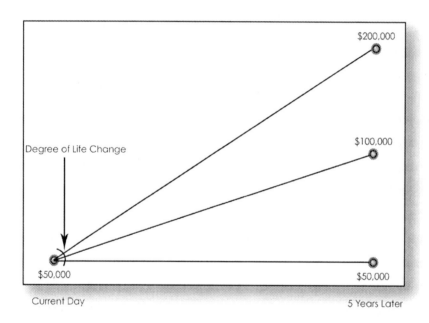

The Joe Verde Group is a global provider of sales and management training. Along with his staff, Joe Verde is growing his company at a rate of 73 percent per annum by putting into practice what he teaches. At the core of this is the mantra "Are we doing the most productive thing possible right now?"

Verde has been in business for nineteen years, and while he is an enormous success today, it was not always so. For years Joe made enough, but just enough. It wasn't until he took a decision to hold himself accountable to several new daily disciplines that Joe began to rise above mediocrity and into the elite.

Fascinated by the success of the JV Group, I attended one of their "managers' meetings." I was stunned by some statistics shared with the group.

Eighty-seven percent of the population has no written goals.

Ten percent write down their personal goals as a yearly obligation.

Just three percent contrast their daily performance to those written goals.

Now these stats are important but not nearly as significant as this next one:

Those three percent make TEN TIMES the income of everyone else.

No matter how much money you currently earn, multiply that by ten and envision what your life could be like. If this alone was the only change you made in your daily routine, think of the future you could create for you and your family beyond what money can earn. Think of all aspects of life; think of life balance.

In the early '90s, I worked an average of seventy hours a week and my annual income was around $30,000. That calculates to $8.25 an hour—if I round up. In just a few years, I surpassed the six-figure mark. I can trace this back to one fundamental change

I made. I decided to turn off the radio and tune into business and personal development cassettes and CDs. My drive times have never been less than forty-five minutes. Hence, with each roundtrip, I acquired one and a half hours of further education. Multiply that by five days a week and it comes to seven and a half hours of learning. Carrying the math a little further, that's almost four hundred hours per year. Not only did my mind expand as a result; so did my wallet. A millionaire friend of mine playfully said, "Money isn't everything but the view is a lot better when you're standing on a thick wallet."

While I have used income as an indicator of success, I could have replaced it with other goals, including educational attainment or relationship success. I do not pretend to be a licensed marriage counselor, but on more than one occasion I've been asked to give counsel to troubled couples. Many, indeed most, could be helped with just a few adjustments in their daily decisions. Austin Vickers, the attorney turned national speaker and corporate coach, provides an alarming stat concerning divorce. Seventy-five percent of men do not kiss their wives goodbye in the morning. According to Vickers's in-depth research, puckering up can change the outcome of most marriages. Adding levity to a serious issue, Vickers says, "You can either kiss your wife—or kiss your house goodbye."

If you have not written down your personal or organizational goals, here is another incentive to do so. In 1995, one of my mentors told me, "Michael, failing to put in print what you say you want to accomplish is an act of treason. You are betraying your potential and sacrificing your allegiance to become all that

38

you can be." I took his advice to heart. From then on I took twenty minutes every day to write down my initiatives. To this day I contrast my daily performance to what I put in print. While there is often much left unfinished, I've gained more momentum than ever before. **I encourage everybody to dare to compare on a daily basis. In terms of income, personal achievement, and corporate success, your rewards will be life-changing**.

2. INDUSTRY COMPARISON

We must continually take inventory of what our competitors are doing.

In early 2001, I consulted with a large pharmaceutical company that wished to enhance its already thriving performance. Happily the results were very positive. Two years later I received a call from another global pharmaceutical company that asked me to come aboard to perform the same kind of consultation.

The call came from an executive who had worked for the first drug company back in 2001. She wanted similar help with her new employer. Due to the fact they were in the same industry, I expected to find the same kind of corporate culture, but I was wrong. At first I couldn't place my finger on why, but then it hit me. The first company was proactive and the second, reactive. It was no surprise then that the first company had called me two years earlier. In today's global economy, you can't be two years behind your competition, not when it comes to customer service and leadership ability. This fact was clearly reflected in the share prices of the two drug companies.

To protect ourselves from falling behind, we have to make a strong commitment to knowing what our competitors are doing at all times. We have to make sure they're in our rear-view mirror, not out in front. This does not mean we must spend the bulk of our time studying or copying them, but a frequent strategic glance every now and then is vital—not just a glance at their stock evaluation or current revenue, but more importantly, we must monitor their level of customer service. I made this point to a boardroom full of executives at a large resort/hotel company, and one top manager said he believed that as long as they worked to perfection, they need not worry about the competition. "What defines perfection?" I asked.

Perfection is limited to what we know is possible. If your competition really expands creatively, then what you believe is perfect may soon be outdated. Perfect, by last year's standard, is this year's underperformance.

A championship race car of the '90s, while still in perfect condition, will yield sadly disappointing results in a 2007 race. Similarly I know of several companies that excelled in their retail stores over the past five years but failed to see the advancement their competitors were making with internet sales. They had a proven strategy but failed to react quickly to the growing online market. At the same time, when a company puts all of its efforts into online sales and ignores its walk-in customers, disaster can quickly follow.

The basic lesson, even in the rapidly changing hi-tech marketplace, is to always measure your performance. If you and your competitor are both "perfect," then how do you take market share away from them? As I've written in an earlier chapter, far too many businesses are satisfied with being adequate or average when it comes to customer service, while only a few strive to become different and truly outstanding. The key is intelligent and continual comparison.

My staff and I travel about forty-two weeks a year. I decided to forfeit our frequent-flyer miles, rental car, and hotel points so that we could experience the differences between six companies in each sector. We concentrated on:

Airline Comparisons

1. American Airlines
2. America West (US Airways)
3. Continental
4. Delta
5. Southwest
6. United

Rental Car Comparisons

1. Alamo
2. Avis
3. Budget
4. Enterprise
5. Hertz
6. National

Hotel Comparisons

1. Hampton
2. Hilton
3. Holiday Inn
4. Hyatt
5. Marriott
6. Sheraton

Of course many of these companies evaluate their performance using resources like *Forbes, Money Magazine,* Gallup and J.D. Powers and the U.S. Department of Transportation. And, of course, as I've written previously, acquiring the status of number one does not necessarily mean you're *distinctively* different or have *exceptional* customer service!

In fact, I've attended more than one corporate strategy session where the topic of discussion was how to win high scores on these surveys by finding loopholes in the process—or even how to encourage those making the survey to give great marks even if the experience was unsatisfactory (if not agonizing!). At one such meeting, the general manager trained her associates to recite the following begging script: "Even though you [the consumer] have had a bad experience with someone else on our staff, this survey is a reflection on me. My bonus and job are based on the overall scores, including the sections that have nothing to do with my interaction with you. So please give me high remarks on everything."

Sound familiar? How can a company expect to deal with reality if the surveys returned are fraudulent? How can a leader gain his employees' respect when teaching them to recite such a miserable and dishonest script?

After the meeting I asked the GM to consider this question: How does this behavior actually look to your customers? She replied that she had no choice. So a week later I actually asked a group of her customers at a focus group to share their experiences. What happened when dealing with a member of her staff during the survey process? How had it made the customers feel?

Sixty-three percent reported being asked to not give honest answers but perfect scores for the sake of an employee's job. When we asked them how this made them feel, we got a host of responses. These ranged from "cheated," "dirty," "untruthful," "bribed," "mad," and "confused" to "belittled." They did not feel as if they were dealing with a respectable organization. They did not walk away from the experience feeling as if the company cared about them or about making true progress. One customer said, "Other than them getting a false sense of accomplishment though fabricated scores, I can see no purpose for returning the survey. Why do they make us fill out a survey if they don't want the truth?"

Several companies who participate in such practices have pointed out to me that they did so because of the "scoring matrix." It seems that many survey companies use a system called "top box" scoring. In this method, while a survey may have a rating system of one to five, the survey company or manufacturer only acknowledges a five—the "top box"—as a passing grade. Anything less is considered failure. On top of that, the manufacturer supplying the goods to the retailer will suspend money or inventory allotment should the retailer fail to acquire enough top boxes on their surveys. Like the employee fighting for a job, the retailer is fighting for money and inventory in order to stay in business.

So I approached the manufacturers to inquire about the efficacy of a top-box scoring system. Not surprisingly, only a few bothered to respond to my questions (with the condition they remain anonymous). All said, to one degree or another, "Wall Street offers us no alternative." It seems that investors look at these national customer service rankings as an indicator of how well individual companies are doing. "If we want to continue to see our stock rise, we need these scores. It's not pretty, but it's necessary to survive."

This pressure to win top-box scores on the surveys actually prevents authentic measurement based on a real comparison of customer service in our country's retail industries. Such comparisons require that you complete a transaction in person to truly establish how well a company is performing. With this in mind, we decided to conduct our own survey. And what a difference it made!

We found that in most cases, other than logos and uniform colors, companies were offering almost identical levels of customer service. Even those who ranked high on national surveys failed to deliver an experience that was noticeably different or better than their competitors who ranked lower. Here are the seven categories we used in our independent survey, categories we affectionately called "the simple seven":

Smile
Wait time

Tone of voice
Ease of process
Phone operator response
Facility/equipment cleanliness
Display of consumer empathy

Intentionally, we used a down-to-earth scale to evaluate each category:

0	for appearing uninterested
5	for being ordinary
15	for enthusiastic

Uninterested simply meant the employee processed our transaction as if we were an inconvenience or mechanical process to be completed.

Ordinary speaks for itself. If they processed our transaction with the same attitude and proficiency as the majority, they received five points.

Enthusiastic did not mean they had to do anything extreme or extravagant, but they appeared happy and conveyed sincere appreciation.

After ten visits per company, per traveler, just three companies surfaced at the top of our lists by earning marks in the enthusiastic category. Only one of the eighteen earned the dubious honor of being generally uninterested, with staff often showing real displeasure at having to deal with the public. So that left us with fifteen companies, their national rankings aside, who were conducting business in an "adequate" but unexceptional manner. Note that our modest survey had nothing to do with profitability or stock price. We focused solely on the experience of the customer in order to determine which companies were truly performing an exceptional service.

How beneficial would it be for every company to conduct a survey of its leading competitors? Send ten to fifteen people out and record (preferably using hidden video) their experience. What if more CEOs or owners made a point of using their competitors' service in order to contrast it with their own company's performance? You don't need to contract an outside source to conduct a national survey. Just begin by examining your own personal experiences.

3. Ultimate Possibility Comparison

Don't forget to compare today's reality to tomorrow's opportunity.

A successful company needs to know what is ultimately possible in all areas of customer service. Take airline reservations, for example. Not only should airlines compare their reservations staff to other airlines, but they should also compare it to any company in any industry that practices great phone skills. Why not contrast your operators with the operators at Disney? Think of what's ultimately possible! Contrast your performance with it.

Southwest did not create a reputation for being fun because they saw how much fun other airlines were offering back in the 1990s. QuikTrip and Wawa convenient stores didn't create a mystery shop program because their direct competitors had them. **Those companies acted because they were not content to wait on the beach, not afraid to swim out beyond the daily breakers of their**

industries. They looked to the horizon, regarding business as a large ocean in which every company must do more than just tread water in order to survive and prosper.

Titan Pest Control is one of my smaller clients but one of my most committed to progress. Aaron and Debbie, the owners, think beyond "small company" or even pest control. As owners they share a desire to become all they can be. If that means going outside the box, so be it. Once a week they have a working luncheon with their technicians and office staff to discuss areas for improvement and performance that deserves to be celebrated. Not too many pest control companies practice such a weekly habit, but Titan Pest Control is not an ordinary pest-control company. That's why they have grown very quickly in comparison to their direct competition.

Aaron and Debbie are open-minded and solicit ideas that work for any company. Recently I recorded the after-hours voice messages used by Titan, by several other pest-control companies, and by a few companies outside their industry, companies that offer exceptionally good phone messages. After listening to the robotic, predictable recordings, Aaron wanted to be as good, if not better, than the ones who stood out, regardless of industry. "Our customers deserve the very best service we can give them."

Who does your company compare itself to? How often do you notice when someone performs a service exceptionally well? Imagine the results if a rental car company compared their customer service to a company like Mastro's Steakhouse, which is known for superior service? What if a car salespersons' income depended on tips rather than commissions? What if airport security screening personnel were required to provide the kind of courtesy and helpfulness you routinely find in Nordstrom's department stores or Chick-fil-A fast-food restaurants? No doubt the pilots, attendants, and security guards would smile a lot more than they do now. And so would we, the passengers.

The possibilities are almost endless. What if an insurance company answered their phones with as much enthusiasm as Southwest Airlines? What a difference it would make if your grocery store took on Disney's attitude that every employee is a cast member in a living pageant that was creating wonderful memories for consumers. Absurd? Perhaps, but so was the idea of a fun airline before Southwest made it happen.

Truly creative thinking requires both passion and purposeful planning. Most companies can't think outside the box of their "squared-off" thinking. Many can't look out to the horizon. The few that can, however—what a difference they make! And usually they don't do anything all that new or outlandish but earn the gratitude and loyalty of consumers by being brilliant at the basics. **In today's fast-changing marketplace, being committed to a handful of basic principles while keeping your eyes on the limitless opportunities of the future is enough to earn you the honor of being the very best in your business.**

Part Four

SO SIMPLE IT'S DIFFICULT

Four Basic Steps to Extraordinary Service

In the '90s I was commissioned to research organizations that had established a reputation for great customer service. At numerous consumer focus groups in California and Arizona, we asked "What five companies with great service come to mind?" The names mentioned most often were Southwest Airlines, Disney, Marriott, Starbucks, and In and Out Burger.

We then began to look for commonalities. Four different factors soon became evident. In each case I was amazed to discover that success did not arise from anything extreme or extravagant. It simply came down to the basics.

Herb Kelleher, the extroverted former president of Southwest Airlines, was a focal point in our research. He responded to one question by saying "The secret to Southwest's success is so simple most people can't figure it out." It was the dedicated execution of a handful of basic actions. The fact that these actions are so obvious explains why so few realize their importance. They are simply the four timeless principles of modern customer service—performed well. As a consumer and research analyst, I've learned that successful organizations realize that common sense is not so common a practice. It must be passionately enforced within every corporate culture.

I . THE REASONING

Understanding why is even more important than knowing what to do.

When comparing organizations like In and Out Burger to McDonalds, Marriott to Hampton, Starbucks to It's a Grind, Disney to Six Flags, Southwest to US Airways; we learned many things, but most importantly we learned that the top performers all spent more time on *why* an action was important than on how to perform that action. The *what to do* is like a destination, but the w*hy* is the fuel that gets you there. Companies that deliver a distinctive, pleasurable, even memorable experience are companies that ensure their employees understand this.

Let me give an example. I met Amy Baker, a flight attendant for Southwest Airlines, while seated in 19A. After observing her and the rest of the crew entertain us while serving beverages, I asked why Southwest seems friendly in comparison to most other airlines. She said, "We hire for attitude, train on aptitude and, most importantly, we are expected to have fun. That is after we ensure your safety, of course."

"Why fun?" I asked.

She explained that when fun is in the atmosphere, laughter is soon to follow, which diminishes tensions and encourages communication. It also bonds people together. "Anyone can fly you to your destination, but only Southwest makes the flight itself really desirable." Amy obviously understands *why*. If you happen to be flying as you read this, ask yourself, Is it obvious that this airline trains its staff like Southwest? Or is it obvious they're only going through a routine, checking off each task they perform on a mental list they've memorized but probably don't fully understand?

2. Greeting the Customer

The first basic action is the act of greeting. The reason why it's so vital is that all consumers are in search of importance and purpose. How often do you visit a business and receive an attentive greeting? When I say attentive, I don't mean spastic. I mean a greeting that says, "I'm truly glad you're here."

Before greeting our customers, we should ensure that everyone knows that their first duty when someone arrives is to make them feel important. The feeling of importance is a fundamental need in human beings. Abraham Maslow, a pioneer in the study of human behavior, conducted many studies into what motivates humans to act. He published his findings in a 1943 paper titled "The Theory of Human Motivation." It concluded that at the center of human behavior was a deep need to feel belonging and status in society.

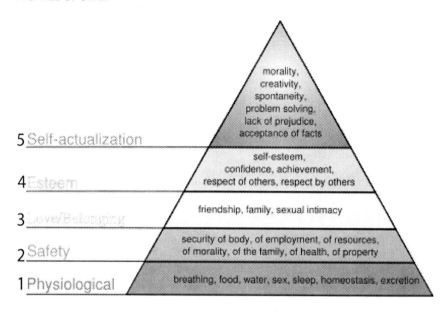

An organization that helps meet this hierarchy of needs can turn a one-time buyer into a returning customer. A customer is not a "good" customer until they return, and a major reason for a customer to return is a feeling of being valued. Greeting them upon arrival with appreciation is the first step to becoming their business of choice. After all, we've not only sold them a product or performed a service; we've given them a sense of worth.

How many places of business greet each consumer in a way that conveys "You're here and we value your presence"? Obviously not many. After thousands of miles of business travel, I can instantly see the difference between employees who know *why* they're greeting me and those who couldn't care less.

There is one airline, for example, on which I often feel like a convict serving time. At the gate, the gruff wardens hold out their hands with a scowl as I hand over my ticket first and later my boarding pass. When I enter the aircraft, the greeting is no better.

Once after such a *"Con Air"* flight, I turn on the hotel TV and there is the company's latest commercial, promising to be the airline that cares. Now I'm not expecting a red carpet and free caviar, but a pleasant hello might even convince me to fly with them again sometime.

In all my fifteen years of working (training, consulting, sometimes even transforming) organizations, I have found that most owners and executives understand the importance of a warm greeting. Yet they themselves too often fail to set a convincing example with their own employees.

In 2005, I conducted a two-day seminar with the executive and management team of a global company. On day one we discussed the importance of first impressions. Everyone agreed that no one should ever encounter a customer without greeting them. Furthermore, we defined *customer* as anyone we encounter, including fellow employees and vendors. One top executive prominently stood up and vowed, "We cannot just give attention to those who appear to have an open wallet. We must treat everyone with respect. A good greeting is the first sign of appreciation."

When it was time for lunch, I led the team out of the boardroom. Near the elevator we passed the mailman, and I said hello. At the bus I turned and faced the eager group (they were ready for lunch) and said, "Let me ask you a question. Your answer will determine whether or not you get on board. Should we greet everyone we meet?"

Like marines, they responded "YES, SIR!"

"Out of the forty-seven of you, how many greeted the mailman?"

Like a congregation realizing they had just let down their pastor, their chins fell to their chests. Acting the part of Reverend Mike, I playfully said they were forgiven. "But let not thy experience pass thou by without first learning its valuable lesson." It was a two-day conference and when, by chance, we encountered the mailman the next day, needless to say, it was comical as forty-eight people (myself included) made certain he knew he was appreciated. Again, at the bus, I said, "Who do you think he'll think of the next time he goes shopping for a product we offer?" My flock of converts all nodded as if to say amen.

One corporate excuse for poor customer service that I've often heard over the years is that "We can't find good help." To this I now respond with three questions, each followed with a bit of common sense:

"Do we make our expectations clear before hiring?"

If we don't, they'll determine what we get.

"Do we demonstrate the kind of the behavior we expect from staff?"

We attract what we project.

If I get an affirmative on both accounts, I ask,

"To what extent do we reward and discipline?"

If you don't inspect what you expect, and don't discipline neglect, then complacency is what you accept. It's called accountability.

Indeed, by comparing the performance of other local organizations, you can verify that good people are available in the same zip code. It would be easy for Starbucks, Chick-fil-A, Discount Tire Company, QuikTrip convenience stores, and the In and Out burger chain to all adopt the same negative thinking. They all deal with the same demographics and must overcome the same hiring obstacles.

Visit any In and Out Burger and you'll be amazed at the consistency of service at all 175-plus locations across the western United States. They understand that if you supply a quality product, a clean premises, and friendly service, you can trump the competition. We found several locations where the golden arches of McDonalds shared the same intersection as the golden arch of In and Out. But, while they may occupy the same neighborhood, McDonalds does not enjoy the same cult-like following of In and Out. The lines at In and Out often look like those at a new Disneyland ride: literally encircling the building.

Unlike McDonald's ever-changing menu, In and Out only serves burgers, shakes, and fries. Their reputation is built on fresh food and a "Happy you're here!" greeting. One of their team leaders said it would be easy to blame complacent service on bad hiring circumstances rather than to accept responsibility. "But then I wouldn't be a leader in our company, nor even an employee," she assured me.

To be fair, In and Out pays their people well. In our ten-store survey, employees averaged $1.22 more an hour. How can they pay that and remain so profitable? By shifting their marketing dollars to where it matters most: to the people who provide the service. Not to an outside agency, which will come up with a new jingle about "loving" service. Makes common sense, right? At In and Out, word of mouth takes care of much of the marketing.

I believe that every organization needs to imbue its culture with the importance of sincere, friendly greetings. The leaders must set the example in this and highlight the reasons *why*. Our job begins by helping people to feel valued in our presence. Consumers who feel an increase in self-worth become our advocates. The more advocates we have, the greater the worth of our company.

At my own company, we began to heighten our customer sensitivity. At the onset we were encouraged to keep in mind that, when doubtful, it was important to recall the examples set by companies like Marriott, Starbucks, Nordstrom's, Midwest Express, Southwest Airlines, In and Out Burger, Discount Tire Company, and QuikTrip and Wawa convenience stores.

Each and every encounter with these companies may not be outstandingly pleasant, but more times than not we left their business feeling good about ourselves, and about them. Naturally we told our friends. This was exactly how we hoped our own clients would feel.

3. Thanks

Like greetings, expressing appreciation for someone's business is a simple but sorely underdeveloped skill. At the end of most transactions, we're given a perfunctory thank you. It's obviously more habit than honesty. As with greetings, the reason why employees fail to display authentic appreciation for a consumer's business is rooted in their lack of understanding.

Thank you is so important because, if convincing, it ensures the customer knows that _we know_ that he or she had a choice. And we're very glad they chose us.

This is one of the most important tasks of any retail job: conveying to every customer that we appreciate their choice. Yet few companies ever make this clear to their employees. It ought to be made clear even before an employee is hired, during the interview itself. If the prospective employee can't grasp this, he or she shouldn't get the job.

I make my home in Phoenix, but as I write this chapter I'm in a cabin near Flagstaff. Earlier Gretta (our faithful Golden Retriever) and I jumped in the Jeep and visited the Starbucks in town. As I took my first sip of the nectar of life (Grande, Mocha, extra shot, no-fat, no-whip), the barista said, "Thanks, Michael. Hope you have an amazing day."

For $4.25 I received not only a jolt to my consciousness but also genuine recognition of my patronage. I felt as if, when I heard my name, he wanted me, individually, to feel my visit was appreciated. We've come to expect a cashier to convey some polite gratitude for our money, but from a multi-tasking brew-master? But this is the norm at Starbucks. Uniquely, the company makes a point of highlighting our purchase. And I only spent $4.25. Where else do you find, for this price, this kind of personal attention?

What about your own business? When did you last convey your sincere appreciation for a customer's patronage? Companies like Starbucks, Southwest, and QuikTrip have taught us how important this is. And, while it is vital to monitor how our employees are performing in this regard, it's even more important to keep reminding them *why* we demand this.

Every customer, every time, needs to know that *we know* they had a choice and we're glad they chose us. An employee who delivers that message is raising our business above the competition.

4. Tone of Voice

When I was conducting training seminars for successful Harley Davidson dealer Rick Hatch, he asked an interesting question. "Michael, if your life depended on customer service and you had to concentrate on only one aspect of this, what would it be?"

"Tone of voice," I responded without hesitation. If there is a tipping point for award-winning service, it is tone of voice.

Many organizations teach their people about various aspects of customer service, but often this "training" is too rehearsed, too robotic. At Performance Architects, we call this "mechanical hospitality." A business may go through the motions of greeting and thanking, but because they fail to emphasize the *why*, everything gets turned into a mechanical process. For example, many local grocery stores fail to match Safeway's ability to express sincere appreciation. Just imagine you are the third person back in an express checkout line. The first person steps up to the counter and *click*.

"Welcome to ABC Grocery. Will that be cash or check? Debit or credit? Paper or plastic? Thank you and have a nice day."

The line moves forward. *Click.*

"Welcome to ABC Grocery. Will that be cash or check? Debit or credit? Paper or plastic? Thank you and have a nice day."

Now it's your turn. *Click.*

"Welcome to ABC Grocery. Will that be cash or check? Debit or credit? Paper or plastic? Thank you and have a nice day."

Did you manage not to scream?

Without a convincing tone of voice, service becomes systematic, unsympathetic, ineffective, and even hostile. **Tone of voice is the single most important aspect of customer interaction.**

Many training hours have been wasted teaching people scripts because scripts have a way of inducing routines that leave the consumer feeling more like a number than an important customer. Teaching scripts can be necessary and effective if—and this is a big if—we first focus on delivery. The words we speak only account for 7 percent of the message we convey. Tone of voice accounts for 38 percent. If at the end of a phone conversation with my wife I quickly say "I-luv-ya" (as if it's one word), I get the same in return. But if I slow down and affectionately say "I love you," even though I used the same words, her response is very different.

Without a doubt, tone of voice is the most critical factor in expressing genuine appreciation for a customer, employee, spouse, or child. In today's aggressive marketplace, being good equates to being average, and average is simply not good enough to win anyone's loyalty. To be elevated to the status of provider of choice, you must spark a consumer's enthusiasm. Interestingly, the definition of *enthusiasm* is: "something that arouses a consuming interest." (dictionary.com) In order for our consumers to be "aroused," we must show them that we're consumed—not bored—by their presence. And while that sounds like a tall order, remember our ability to be brilliant in the basics is what produces enthusiastic loyalty.

Talk about, train, and explain the importance of good tone of voice. The moment you stop is the moment you begin to slip back into "adequate" service. Again, products and services must be present and expectations met, but the most powerful tool you have in your journey to the peak of success is tone of voice.

One question I'm often asked is, "Why is tone of voice more important than body language?" Intuitive math wizards suggest that if words make up 7 percent and tone of voice, 38 percent, that leaves 55 percent for body language. My reasoning is simple: tone of voice is the tipping point. Tone of voice brings with it certain attentiveness. Show me good tone of voice and I'll show you, more often than not, good body language. The opposite is not always true. A manager from Marriott simplified the need for good tone of voice by saying, "It is easy to pose like an actor, but tone of voice breathes life into the character."

5. PHONE SKILLS

I am always shocked by the gap between advertising commitment and phone-skill development. The stack of money spent by companies on advertising might reach into outer space, but if we dug a hole into the deep corporate commitment to phone skills, we would barely have a small divot. Shelly Langston, successful magazine owner, says, "We love making the phone ring for the business that advertises with us. But, in the end, the sale must be made by the voices of those who own the number."

Mrs. Langston is not only dedicated to producing a high-quality magazine; she also spends her own time and money training clients about effective customer service and phone skills. She emphasizes capturing the attention and respect of the caller. The hype of advertising can hypnotize our attention and put us in a trance in which we think only about possible big returns but fail to focus on execution.

Thank goodness after researching and observing Marriott, they woke me from my trance. I learned that advertising without good phone skills is like Pinocchio trying to bluff at liars' poker.

You can advertise faster, better, friendlier service, and yet, upon answering the call, your worthless cards are shown. I dare you to pick up the phone, as we did, and call five airlines, rental car agencies, hotel chains, car dealerships, banks, and cellular phone and insurance companies. Then rank your experiences into two columns: adequate/average and pleasant/attentive. Now do the same for you and your industry competitors. Most likely you already know the outcome. At least you should know.

As I've written, our ability to escalate profits and establish market-share dominance depends on being outstanding at the basics. If your competitor is still under the influence of their own hypnotic advertising, they fail to notice their own robotic, mediocre phone skills.

Here again, tone of voice is all-important. Yes, you need to provide information and perhaps follow a particular script, but a good tone of voice comes first—always. This is something your competitors will probably never understand until it proves to be the Achilles' heel in their futile attempts to compete.

We also need to be sure to teach that, while the race may be on to answer a call, "ThankyouforcallingXYGhowmayIhelpyou?" as if it's one word; is a useless introduction. When we rush through the message, all we convey is "I have little time for you. You're not someone I value. You're just a process to be completed. Why did you have to interrupt my chatting anyway?"

Take care of a caller by enthusiastically thanking them, stating the company or department you represent, and providing your name. After I urged an audience of office receptionists to adopt these common-sense rules, an executive administrative assistant said in exasperation, "But I just don't have the time!" The audience nodded in agreement. I acknowledged that their job was very demanding (not to mention undervalued) and said that I understood their frustration. But I then asked for a participant to time me as I demonstrated two ways of responding to a call.

First:

"XYZ Insurance?"

Then:

"Thank you for calling XYZ Insurance. This is Michael. How can I help you?"

The first greeting took 0.9 seconds and the second greeting lasted 1.8. The difference in time is minuscule, but the difference in impact is monumental. A mentor once said, "Sometimes we unconsciously elevate the truth to make ourselves feel more important, or to subliminally inform people we feel underappreciated."

The main reason *why* we answer the phone is not, despite popular opinion, to answer questions or to give information. Our first goal should be to convince the caller that they've called someplace that is truly distinctive—someplace that cares and has concern for everyone as an individual.

Sure, it may be necessary to have a recording, but please toss away the antiquated "You're call is important to us; all calls are answered in the order received" recorded tagline. During one focus group, we asked what most people thought about calling a certain company. Wow! It was as if we'd thrown a bleeding sirloin steak to a pack of hyenas. They went after that question with carnivorous vengeance. As we maneuvered our way through their fangs and claws, we determined that it was the blatant lack of effort—particularly in post-sales service—that had driven them into a frenzy.

One man recounted listening to a salesperson talk about the benefits of purchasing a warranty and promising award-wining service. "Okay," the customer said, and asked for a brochure. On his cellular speakerphone, he dialed the printed number and together he and the salesperson listened to the wretchedly poor, recorded phone message provided by the warranty company. Another attendee asked, "Why is it every company seems to use the same recording? If my call is so important, why isn't someone there to answer it in reasonable time?"

Mark Sanborn—consultant, author, and popular speaker—makes the following definitive statement about phone skills: "The difference between status quo and full potential is always the difference between common knowledge and consistent application." We simply need to apply common sense to every call. Answer quickly, introduce enthusiastically, and convey sincerity.

So there you have them, the four basic steps to outstanding service: good greetings, sincere thanks, authentic tone of voice, and gracious phone skills. So simple, so easy to take for granted, yet so very important to every company's success.

PART FIVE

THE LEADERSHIP PARADOX

The height of an organization stands in direct proportion to its leaders' influence and curiosity.

Happy customers, committed talent, and rising profits are euphoric signs for ambitious executives and owners. While it's possible to experience all three in unison, from time to time only very strong leadership can produce these year after year. Leaders who create strong organizational cultures have a paradoxical ability to connect directly with those they lead while remaining far enough ahead to *inspire*. Outstanding leaders are not common. Too many are either so removed from the people they lead that they become mere figureheads or so close that they can't get out in front to lead. Within this paradox of leadership, we find two key qualities that a great leader must possess.

One, the ability to exert powerful influence both horizontally and vertically within an organization.

Two, an insatiable curiosity.

I often meet with executives and owners who possess one or the other of these two qualities, but seldom do I find leaders who display both to an extraordinary degree. When both are present, outstanding execution is evident.

1. INFLUENCE

Hope is the key to every future success.

Options can be your best friend, your greatest equity. The more options you have in life, the less tension you experience. Your back is never against the wall. In managing people, however, options can be a source of exasperation.

Leaders who manage by dictatorship gain compliance via intimidation. While a democracy is not always desirable in business, a dictatorship usually fails because most people, in today's economy, have options. Unless their options have been removed, talented people often flee when a dictator aggressively restricts their expression.

A leader who understands how to gain voluntary consent is a leader who has true influence and power. The best definition of leadership was given to me by Gray McDougal, a successful general manager for a multi-million-dollar corporation. He said,

"Leadership is about the ability to get others to do something you want done, but in such a way that they want to do it."

While McDougal's first name suggests something smudged between black and white, that's hardly Gray's true description. He is black or white in everything he does, but with a clear focus on what is and is not acceptable. He knows that he must communicate so that his people not only respect him but also fully agree with him. You'll find the same leadership ability in people such as Jack Welch at GE, Warren Buffet at Berkshire Hathaway, Howard Schultz at Starbucks, Herbert D. Kelleher at Southwest, Fred Smith at FedEx, and Chester Cadieux at QuikTrip. They may not be mirror images of McDougal's personality, but they do share the same ability to earn the respect and eager contribution of their employees. With respect comes influence, and the influence of all these leaders is now legendary.

How many leaders do you know personally that have the same ability? How many do you know with influence both up and down the corporate hierarchy and side to side across the executive and board levels? How many more do you know who seem to lack this influence? How does your own leadership compare? If you know someone who has the admiration of the masses (or if you yourself are such a person), review all the traits of their leadership style. You'll most likely come up with the same key quality that we did.

Emotional intelligence (EQ) is one of the most important elements in gaining influence. EQ is the intelligent management of human emotions, both internal and external. Knowing how to manage your own emotions while influencing the emotions of others is

EQ. Whether it is done with natural talent or is a long-practiced skill, a high EQ is vital for successful leadership.

A good leader always thinks, Will what I'm going to say or do have the best chance of working both short and long term? That is, does it have the best odds of igniting emotions and, as a result, improving the performance of those whom I need to achieve my goals for the company?

Too often people blurt out things that make them feel smart or prove they're right, but these things may have little chance of actually working. I've seen overzealous owners and mangers make demands and expect immediate compliance, and while no employees disagreed, many soon quit. They may not have physically left, but in their performance and their attitude, they quit.

In my early years of management, I told a lot of people exactly what I thought to try to prove that I was right and in some cases prove they were wrong. In the end my direct honesty created little or no momentum in my career. The result was an inability to gain influence. The reason for my lack of influence was my unwillingness to channel my thoughts and actions through the thought processes and emotions of those I needed to agree with me. I'm not talking about politics nor am I launching a crusade for people to say only what seems friendly. I am talking about intelligence-about EQ. Advice from Jack Welch suggests that is a colossal mistake, but remember too that being candid and "winning" a hollow agreement is often worse than provoking a solid disagreement. At least the latter could produce a constructive dialogue.

"Michael," a mentor once said, "before going into the boardroom, one you know will be thick with opposing opinions, picture yourself and others as magnets. You are all repelling each other in opposite directions. Your goal should be to say what you need to say so that all those magnets flip over in the same direction. So that they can't help be first attracted, then attached, to your point of view. You can't force attachment. If you try, they'll move away from you at the first opportunity. The more tension we create to get someone to agree, the greater their resolve to oppose you. When new options arise, they'll take off."

He added, "Of course, if they present facts that alter your own opinion, you must be willing to flip yourself." As crazy as it may sound, for months I sometimes placed two magnets in my pocket before entering a discussion I knew would contain opposing views.

Another key factor in gaining influence is hope. In corporate America hope can sometimes sound too soft. It's a word that may denote people who wander in tranquil fields, counting daisies while singing "If I could teach the world to sing."

In reality hope is a weapon—a weapon that enables you, ultimately, to win new market-share. Put hope in the hearts and minds of people and they will be inspired with new determination to perform well.

Think of hope as a real competitive advantage. Hope by definition is "the feeling that what is wanted can be had or that events will turn out for the best. To believe, desire, or trust." (dictionary.com) An employee who trusts his leader's words are true and his goals are correct is actually a great competitive advantage for a company. An enthusiastic, dedicated corporate culture is one of the most important factors in determining an organization's future performance.

One of the predominant reasons why Apple, GE, and Google are at the forefront of their industries is the hopeful quality of their cultures. Google's co-founders, Larry Page and Sergey Brin, grew their business from a tiny start-up to more than 5,000 talented employees. And they continue to attract the brightest young talents in their industry because of Google's reputation for being fun-loving, high-performing, innovative, and above all, its hopeful prospects for continuing leadership in the fast-changing Internet information sector. Take away such enthusiastic hope and Google would soon become mediocre, average, common.

John Maxwell, the noted speaker, is credited with saying, **"Where there is no hope in the future, there is no power in the present."** Take a look at those around you who are full of gloom and doom, whose performance is merely adequate. Those are the same people with little sense of hope, little passion to perform and, in extreme cases, even to live.

When my job requires that I intervene in resolving a conflict, one of my first objectives is to determine where hope is missing. I do the same when dealing with a company with a high turnover of staff. To the degree that one has hope, one has perseverance to overcome almost anything. Take Southwest Airlines for example. Facing the same market difficulties and rising fuel costs as other airlines, how often do you see Southwest employees picketing?

A fly on the wall at Southwest would reveal that while not everyone agrees about everything, everyone does hope that together they'll find a way to work out their difficulties.

Earlier in this book, I mentioned Amy Baker from Southwest. She was very upbeat and proud of her airline. Angela (I'll save her job by omitting her last name) is a different story. She works for a larger airline, and her outlook is altogether different from Amy's. In her view, her employer cares about only one thing: profit. And because she has little hope of that ever changing, she awaits an opening at Southwest. She's not alone.

We conducted research to determine which airline, if given a choice, most job applicants would ideally join. We advertised free resume preparation for anyone wanting to work for an airline. When asked which airlines they would prefer to work for, Southwest was overwhelmingly the employer of choice. At the core of this was the fact of Southwest's hope-inspiring commitment to its customers and its staff, as well as its future profits. Even when we asked if a dollar more an hour could sway their first choice, many still chose Southwest. That's true corporate leadership, and power—power the other birds wish they possessed.

To create hope in an organization, leaders must set expectations that can actually be met. Hope must be based on solid achievement, not pipe dreams, advertising jingles, or dictatorial delusions. With the delivery of what was promised, hope is manifested.

Case in point: I was involved with a company that had four divisions, each with its own hiring manager. All four were in the same line of business, offered a similar pay scale, and shared virtually the same demographics. Yet three of the four had high staff turnover rates. My responsibility was to find out why one was better than the other three. As the research began, I quickly noted that the solicitation of job applicants was the same but after that the high performer deviated from the norm. One glaring difference: only they would honestly state the conditions of employment that were sure to be seen or felt.

The other three made bold promises of high commissions, flexible schedules, advanced training, great management, and of course "a sense of family." To a degree some of these benefits were possible, but not nearly to the extent the recruiting manager passionately proclaimed. We conducted voluntary post-termination interviews and quickly found that the primary reason for leaving was that former employees felt they had been manipulated from the start. They had little faith that the company would ever turn out to be anything close to what they had once hoped it would be.

2. CURIOSITY

Like the ability to influence, leaders must continually grow their curiosity. Curiosity leads to research, research leads to new understanding, and new understanding leads to greater opportunities for growth.

If there is one thing that decelerates an organization's pursuit of its full potential, it's a leader who isn't open to learning as much as possible about his business, indeed his world. Often during a conference, I'll ask the "learners" in the audience to raise their hands. Obviously the majority quickly and proudly put their hands aloft. "Allow me to rephrase the question this way," I say. "How many of you have a reputation for being a learner?" Their faces normally go blank as they rack their brains for a memory that matches this request. Agreeing that learning is important is not the same thing as being an active learner, full of curiosity and hungry for new information.

Most people consider themselves learners. But ask them what they've read or researched; what seminar they've attended recently or what instructional CD have they listened to. Many can't come up with a single example. A friend of mine, who is a famous public speaker, once said, "Trainers, speakers, and teachers are often the hardest to teach." Similarly, I think, many managers, executives, and owners are difficult pupils. Yet those providing direction for others have a duty to expand their own knowledge, to test their wits and exercise their curiosity about the changing world we live in.

Unfortunately too few leaders participate in continual research and discovery. This is a lesson I learned the hard way. After taking over as sales director for a division that had for years earned an average of $120,000 in annual sales, I boosted sales to a quarter of a million. I was satisfied and the executive team was ecstatic. Then one day, while seated in my rich leather high-back chair I was visited by the CEO. He interrupted my pompous disposition to tell me about his recent trip to Houston Texas. He had met with another sales director who, in the same business, recorded 30 percent higher revenues than ours.

Noting my attempt to diffuse his excitement by questioning the truth of those figures, he said that people had thought the same thing when I boosted sales. He challenged me to find ways to rise to the next level. I told him I was already extremely busy and doing everything I knew how to do!

"Therein lies the problem," he responded. "You're doing all that you currently know how. In your current state of mind, you can't see that perhaps your hectic schedule is due to not learning how to become more effective and efficient. Maybe you should admit there's more to learn." I was naive then but not totally stupid. I knew he was right. So I began to pursue the knowledge I needed to grow the business once again.

That lesson was initially painful, but in the end it taught me the need to remain constantly open to new information. Had I done so, I would have been telling my boss about all the new ways I'd discovered to increase our profit and production, not complaining about my hectic schedule. Once I took on the role of student, my staff began to see me, their leader, as an active learner. The staff not only followed my lead; their hesitation about suggesting or implementing new processes almost vanished without a trace.

The great basketball coach John Wooden once said, **"It's too late to prepare when the opportunity comes."** With this in mind, when the market shifts and an organization must change, it's too late to wade through the muck of hesitant learners.

The organization that creates a culture of learning is a company with an obvious competitive advantage. When researching GE, we found at the core of their dominance a culture of continuous learning. If there was ever a banquet table where deserving companies were seated to feast on increased profits and production, GE would be seated at its head. This was largely due to the fact that when changes were required, the team at GE was able to respond quickly thanks to their culture of continual learning and adaptation. Indeed GE offers bona-fide training initiatives, whereas many other companies offer, at best, a training facade. Perhaps that's why so many companies have to choke down a deep dish of regret at the end of the year instead of a feast of record profits.

The culture of learning shared by executives at GE is similar to what we know about many of the richest American entrepreneurs. *Forbes* magazine published some interesting facts about billionaires. Many of the richest read between one and two hours a day. Mark Cuban, worth $2.3 billion, reads on average six hours or more a day. Which do you think came first: the billions or the reading habit? Or was it his passion for learning, followed by the billions?

Curiosity is essential to expand the opportunities of any organization. Not only does a leader with a reputation for learning find him- or herself better equipped to face the challenges of a changing economy; this leader sets an important example for his employees to follow—not to mention a towering obstacle for the competition to overcome.

Influence and curiosity: they are not the only ingredients to great leadership, but they are also ingredients common to all great leaders. Sadly one or the other or both, is usually lacking in the least successful managers and executives whom I have encountered over the years. Anyone with the desire to reach their full leadership potential would be wise to increase their ability to influence others and to expand their quest for new knowledge. Combine those two pursuits with the lessons you've learned from my previous chapters and I believe that the definition of success in customer service will always include your name.

FURTHER READING

I'm often asked for the titles of helpful books about leadership and customer service. Here are some great ones that I believe should be in everyone's business library.

Collins, Jim. *Good to Great.* HarperCollins Publishers, Inc., 2001

Welch, Jack and Suzy. *Winning.* HarperCollins, April 2005.

Maxwell, Dr. John C. *Developing the Leader Within You.* Thomas Nelson, 2003.

Boyatzis, Richard, and Annie McKee. *Primal Leadership: The Hidden Driver of Great Performance.* Harvard Business School Press, 2001.

Maltz, Maxwell. *Psycho Cybernetics.* Prentice-Hall (first edition 1960).

Lencioni, Patrick. *5 Dysfunctions of a Team.* Wiley, John & Sons, Incorporated, 2002.

Andrews, Andy. *The Travelers Gift.* Thomas Nelson, 2002.

Johnson, Spencer. *Who Moved My Cheese?* Putnam, 1998.

Blanchard, Ken and Susan Fowler, Laurence Hawkins. *One Minute Manager Meets the Monkey*, Harper Business Essentials 2005.

Godin, Seth. *Purple Cow*. Penguin Books Ltd., 2005.

Gladwell, Malcolm. *Tipping Point*. Back Bay Books, 2002.

Breinigsville, PA USA
13 January 2011
253162BV00002B/105/A